IS IT POETRY

TOSHIKO HIRATA

IS IT POETRY?

Translated from the Japanese
by Eric E. Hyett & Spencer Thurlow

PHONEME
MEDIA

DEEP
VELLUM

DALLAS, TEXAS

Phoneme Media, an imprint of Deep Vellum Publishing
3000 Commerce St., Dallas, Texas 75226
deepvellum.org · @deepvellum

Deep Vellum is a 501c3 nonprofit literary arts organization founded in 2013 with the
mission to bring the world into conversation through literature.

Support for this publication has been provided in part by grants from the National
Endowment for the Arts, the Texas Commission on the Arts, the City of Dallas Office of
Arts and Culture's Arts Activate program, and the University of Chicago Center for East
Asian Studies.

Paperback ISBN: 9781646052738
Ebook ISBN: 9781646052943

LIBRARY OF CONGRESS CATALOGING-IN-PUBLICATION DATA

Names: Hirata, Toshiko, 1955– author. | Hyett, Eric E, translator. |
Thurlow, Spencer, translator. | Hirata, Toshiko, 1955- Shinanoka. |
Hirata, Toshiko, 1955- Shinanoka. English
Title: Is it poetry? / Toshiko Hirata ; translated from the Japanese by
Eric E. Hyett & Spencer Thurlow.
Description: First U.S. edition. | Dallas : Deep Vellum, 2024. | Parallel
text in Japanese and English translation .
Identifiers: LCCN 2023039969 (print) | LCCN 2023039970 (ebook) | ISBN
9781646052738 (trade paperback) | ISBN 9781646052943 (ebook)
Subjects: LCSH: Hirata, Toshiko, 1955---Translations into English. | LCGFT:
Poetry.
Classification: LCC PL852.I6844 A2 2024 (print) | LCC PL852.I6844 (ebook)
LC record available at https://lccn.loc.gov/2023039969
LC ebook record available at https://lccn.loc.gov/2023039970

Cover design by Lexi Earle
Interior layout and typesetting by Andrea García Flores

PRINTED IN CANADA

Contents

Is It Poetry?

一月七日

旅に出よう
詩を書くためにだけ旅に出よう
そう決めたのに一回目から早くも挫折
夕暮れどきの丸ノ内線に
臆面もなく腰掛けている
中吊りの　女性雑誌の広告は
横書きのっピンクの文字が目立つ
わたしとの接点何もなく
じっとみていると
自分が男になった気分

男になろう
旅に出るのが難しいなら
詩を書くためにだけ男になろう
そう決めたわたしの耳に
「寂しいから犬のトルソーを買ったの」という細い声
そおうか　寂しいとき女はトルソーを買うのか
買ったトルソーを抱いて寝るのか
トルソー＝首及び四枝を欠く胴体だけの塑像（広辞苑）
そんなものを買うのが喜びなのか
男のからだも女のからだも
丸ノ内線は等しく運ぶ
けれどもゆれを感じる場所は
ひとりずつ
微妙に違っている

Is It January?

I'm going on a trip.
Just to write poetry.
That was my plan. But right away: setback.
Early evening I steal a seat on the subway;
my eyes fix
on *Elle Japon Monthly*'s
conspicuous pink
dangling ads
that say nothing to me.
Have I turned into a man?

I'm going on this trip.
Even if I have to be a man. Become a man,
literally just to write poetry.
Then, a thin voice:
I bought a Bear Hug Body Pillow because I was lonely.
So that's it! When a woman feels lonely, she buys a "body pillow."
I bet she cuddles that body to sleep.
Body = the torso apart from the head, neck,
arms, and legs: a sculpture of the trunk of the body. (Kōjien
        Dictionary)
I bet she enjoys buying stuff like that.
This subway line transports
men and women equally,
though they feel vibration subtly,
different for each person.

男の駅

女の駅

男の駅

女の駅

電車は順に停車する

男の駅

女の駅

男の駅

女の駅

車体は次第に赤みを帯びる

男の駅

女の駅

男の駅

女の駅

いつしかお客は犬のトルソー

Men's stop

Women's stop

Men's stop

Women's stop

Trains stop in order

Men's stop

Women's stop

Men's stop

Women's stop

Reddish light tinges the Marunouchi Line

Men's stop

Women's stop

Men's stop

Women's stop

Before you know it, every passenger's a Bear Hug Body Pillow.

二月七日

道路工事が終わらない
にせものの太陽の下
男らはきつい目をして
ざらついた
アスファルトの皮を剥ぎ
頑なな肉を堀り起こす
濁った悲鳴が
青ざめた寝台に眠るわたしの
耳をひりひり痛めつける

ヴィンセント・ヴァン・ゴッホ
この国でかつてそう呼ばれたわたし
蟻のような右肩の濁点が
気になって仕方なかったが
鳥にでも啄まれたのか
いつしか濁点は姿を消して
今では
フィンセント・ファン・ゴッホ

ヴィンセント・ヴァン・ゴッホ
濁ったわたしの名前
わたしのこころ
フィンセント・ファン・ゴッホ
頼りないわたしの未来
わたしの目
どうかこれ以上
失うものがありませんように
与えられるものがありませんように

Is It February?

Endless road construction.
Long-faced men
under a fake sun
scrape
asphalt's skin,
dig out stubborn earth.
I try to sleep in my pale bed,
a diffuse scream
slices my ears.

I would call myself
Vincent Van Gogh in this country.
But I'm worried
about those two V's.
In fact, a crow flew in
flecked at them
now
I'm Fincent Fan Gogh

My vast name:
Vincent Van Gogh.
My feelings:
Fincent Fan Gogh.
My Eyes:
a fickle future.
How can I make it so I never
lose anything
again, never gain anything?

きのう読んだ物語の主人公は三十五歳
人工知能の研究者
きょう読んだ新聞には
三十六歳の男が
臓器移植を受けたという記事
なつかしい晩年
その歳にはわたしもまだ生きていて
毎日ひかりと格闘していた
駐車場のかわりに麦畑
排気ガスのかわりにミストラルがあった
三十七歳、四ヶ月
それから先の自分を知らない

わたしがいなくなったあとも
赤や黄色の産声をあげて
絵の具箱のなかに人はうまれる
贋作の生涯
贋作の自分
わたしの腹に今の残る銃弾
医者はそれをポリープというが
ポリープ　柔らかな半濁音を
濁音のわたしは受け入れられない

The main character in the story I read yesterday
is a thirty-five-year-old AI researcher.
In the daily I read today
a thirty-six-year-old man
received an organ transplant.
Van Gogh
was still alive at those nostalgic ages,
daunted by daily sunlight,
wheat fields instead of parking lots
the *mistral* instead of exhaust gas.
He didn't know himself past
thirty-seven years, four months.

Even after I die,
people will be born in painters' toolboxes
crying red and yellow
counterfeit lifetimes
counterfeit selves.
A doctor calls the bullet that remains
in my belly a polyp.
Polyp   Not angry enough, that
soft *p* sound.

三月七日

「水を運ぶ夜」公演前日。
台本作者としてゲネプロに立ち会う。

ゲネラルプローベ
略してゲネプロ
さらに略してゲネともいう
本版通りに照明（あかり）が入り
本版通りに音楽が入り
本版通りの衣裳をつけて
舞台に上がる役者たち

夜の公園　ささやきあう木
よごれた蛇口からみずが滴る
黄色いのぼり棒に光があたる
巨大なジャングルジムが息づき始める
客の姿は客席にまだなく
演出家やスタッフが
自分の立場で舞台を観ている
まるで違うことを考えながら
ひとつの舞台をにらんでいる

ゲネラルプローベ
今なら間に合う
せりふの変更　照明の変更
衣装の変更　演技の変更
でも　本当に変えたいものは
今さら変えることできないものだ

Is It March?

Outdoor production: *Night of the Water Carriers*.
Playwright takes her seat at the final dress rehearsal.

Dress Rehearsal—
Abbreviated: D. R.
Shortened to: D.
The theater lights, on cue.
The sound, on cue.
The costumes, in place.
Actors take their positions on the stage.

The park at night   whispering trees
dirty water drips from faucets
light hits yellow streamers
the giant jungle gym seems to breathe.
Audience seats, empty outlines on the grass.
The director, the crew, and I watch the play
from our own spots
we glare at the same scene,
have separate thoughts.

It's already Dress Rehearsal!
Even now, a single line could be changed
lighting changed
costumes changed   set changed
but   what I want to change
is the one thing I can't.

上演中止！
上演中止！
叫びたい気持ちが高まってくる
稽古場で
繰り返しつぶやかれたであろう台本の不満が
ゲネラルプローベ　あらわになる
上演中止！
上演中止！
上演中止！
上演中止！

（あの、あなた…。）
（もう、それぐらいで…。ここは夜の公園ですし、
日付も変わったことですし…。）
自分の書いたせりふにたしなめられる
日付が変われば公演初日
もう間に合わない
間に合わない　のか？

ゲネラルプローベ
暗闇のなか
台本をふたつに引き裂く
それでも役者は生きていて
こころにもないことを
舞台で
平気で口にする

I have this urge to scream
Stop the play!
Stop the play!
The script isn't working. I'd murmured my worries to myself at
        studio rehearsals,
now all flaws are revealed on Dress Rehearsal night
Stop the play!
Stop the play!
Stop the play!
Stop the play!

(Excuse me . . . I know it's not reasonable but . . .)
(Changes at what level? At this late date? We've booked
the park at night, we've changed the date once . . .)
If we wait until I'm satisfied with my own script,
There'll be
no opening night.
No   opening night

In pitch blackness,
I tear my script in two;
the actors alive
onstage
speak my words
that have no heart.

四月七日

谷川俊太郎のことを考えている
きょうも
きのうも
おとといも。
図書館にいって
谷川俊太郎の本を三冊借りる
日曜の図書館は
平日よりも疲れた顔をしている

バス停前の
いつか入ろうと思っていた喫茶店は
知らないうちにつぶれていた
その瞬にある
いつかいきたいと思っている大杉医院は健在だ
喫茶店より病院のほうが
寿命が長いということなのか

谷川さんの詩集を読み
谷川さんについて少し書く
エッセイをという注文なのに
なぜか行分け詩になってしまう
谷川さんを読んだせいで
からだが行分け詩のリズムに侵されたらしい

Is It April?

I've been thinking about the poet Shuntarō Tanikawa
today
yesterday
the day before.
On Sundays, the library wears
a tired face.
I take out three books
by Shuntarō Tanikawa.

I'd always meant to go
to the bus stop cafe,
but they demolished it.
Next door, Osugi Medical Partners
is still in good condition, a place
I still might go someday.
I guess a clinic lives longer than a coffee shop.

I read Tanikawa.
I write a little about Tanikawa
try an essay, end up
writing line break poetry.
My body invaded
by Tanikawa's rhythm.

おととい
谷川俊太郎を遠目に見た
谷川俊太郎がしゃべるのも聞いた
年を取った人の話は長い
この世にしがみつくようにマイクの前を離れない
谷川さんのスピーチは明るく楽しく簡潔だった
谷川さんはきっとまだ
年寄りになってはいないのだろう

いつか会いたいと思っていた人が先月死んだ
といって特に会いたくない人が
永遠に生きているわけではない
自分は死なない気がするといっていた
宇野千代という人も亡くなった
谷川俊太郎も多分いつかは。
たくさんの追悼文が書かれるだろう
こぞって腕をふるうだろう
一番読みたいのは
谷川さん自身が書いた
明るく楽しく簡潔な追悼文

あと七分できょうも終わる
いいこともなく悪いこともなく
好きでも嫌いでもない一日
きょうも
きのうも
おとといも。
きょうもきのうもおとといも。
谷川俊太郎が片付かないまま
日曜が終わり月曜になる

Day before yesterday,
I saw Shuntarō Tanikawa from afar.
I heard Shuntarō Tanikawa speak.
Getting old can make you go on and on,
never give up the mic
like you're holding onto this world.
Tanikawa's speech was crisp, fun and light.
Tanikawa seemed far from old.

Someone I'd always wanted to meet
died last month,
which doesn't mean that the people I don't want to meet
live forever. Chiyo Uno, author of *I Will Go On
Living*, died.
And someday, Shuntarō Tanikawa too.
Everyone will raise their hands
to write the eulogies.
But the one I most want to read
is the one Tanikawa himself would write:
crisp, fun, and light.

In seven minutes, today will also end.
A day with no likes, dislikes,
nothing good, nothing bad.
Today
Yesterday
The day before.
Today, yesterday, the day before.
Sunday turns to Monday and I'm still not done
with Shuntarō Tanikawa.

五月七日

雨よ降れ、雨よ降れえと空にむかって念じていると
灰色の空からポツポツ降り出した
よかった、これで安眠できるとほっとしたのもつかの間
八時なるとショベルカーが
ガツーンガツーンガツーンガツーン
雨天決行で作業を始める
連休もすんだし
遊んでばかりもいられないのだろう
働け働け　元気いっぱい
ひとの眠りを妨げよう

（居住者客位
（隣接マンション建築のお知らせ
（工事期間中ご迷惑のかかる事態が生じました場合は
（連絡先　　赤丸興産株式会社
（電話　　　三四七六一三ｘｘｘ

「赤丸興産でございます。ただいま留守にしておりますので御用の……

どうにでもなれという気持ちでコンスタンを多めに飲み
服のまま布団に深く潜り込む
雨よ降れ、雨よ降れえ
ショベルカーをどろどろに溶かしてしまえ

Is It May?

A few drops fall from slate clouds;
I look towards the sky
and pray for rain.
Rain means I'll be able to sleep for a little while.
Every day at 8 A.M., the excavator
moves forward rain or shine
gash gash gash gash
ignores holidays: no more playing all the time.
Work! Work like you mean it!
Make sure nobody gets any sleep!

- ATTENTION: ALL RESIDENTS OF ADJACENT BUILDINGS
- Regarding Construction
- If a problem arises during the construction period
- Contact: Akamaru Industries Co., Ltd.
- Telephone: three four seven six dash three x x x

You've reached Akamaru Industries. We are temporarily
unavailable to take your call. Please . . .

I take a ton of sleeping meds
with a feeling of *how do I get used to this*
hunker into my futon, in my clothes.
Rain! Rain! Melt that excavator to a pulp.

「……もしもし

「寝てた?

「……今何時?

「夕方の四時。連休どうしてた?

「ピパを見た。伊勢丹の屋上で

「聞いたことあるな。何だっけ

ピパ、ツメガエル、南米産

粘土のような色をして落ち葉のように薄っぺら

目は点、口は線、全体は平面

水中でただじっとしてる

えさは金魚 生きた金魚を週に二、三匹

このときばかりは素早く動き

たちまち金魚を腹におさめる

「ふうん。今度一緒にピパ見にいこうか

この人の「今度」は実現したことがない

知っているから「そうね」と答える

この人はこちらの様子は訊きたがるくせに

自分のことは話さない

話せない事情があるのだろう

電話を切り 歯ブラシをくわえ

ベランダから解体工事の現場をのぞく

先週までラーメン屋があったところに

二台のショベルカーがいて

一匹の金魚をめぐり

激しく口論している

. . . uhhhhhhhh hello?
Wait, were you sleeping
. . . . . . um, what time is it?
It's four o'clock in the afternoon.
How were your holidays?
I saw the pipas. Downtown.
Oh, right. What exactly are they again?
Suriname Toads. A frog from South America, flat as a fallen
leaf, brown as clay. Its eyes, dots, mouth, a line,
body, a flat plane. And it just sits there in the water,
eating two or three live goldfish per week. That's the only
time it moves at all, when it gobbles the goldfish
into its belly.
Well, let's go see the pipa-pipas together next time.
They act as if they're really interested
but I know this person's next time
never happens, so I say *Sure*.
Maybe there's a reason,
but they never talk about themselves.
I end the call   get my toothbrush
peek from my balcony at the demolition:
where last week
there was a ramen shop,
two excavators
arguing over a goldfish.

六月七日

ゆうべ誰かがやってきて
泊めてほしいとつぶやいた
ためらいもせず部屋にあげ
ドアを閉めると
二重にカギをかけた

その人は白いシャツを着て
汗をかいているのに震えている
冷たい飲み物と
あったかい飲み物
両方出すと
冷たい方を選んで
一気に飲んだ
それからベッドに倒れ込んだ

この日がくるのを待っていた
この人がいつか　ひとを殺して
匿ってほしいといってやって来る日を
そしたら命がけでこの人を守ると
何年か前　こころに決めた
この日のために引っ越しもせず
電話番号も変えなかった

Is It June?

Last night, someone came to my door
whispering *Can I stay?*
Breathless, I let him in
double locked the door
behind us.

He was sweating,
shivering through a white shirt.
I set out
cold drinks
hot drinks
and he took the cold
in one gulp
collapsed on the bed.

I'd been waiting for the day
when he'd kill someone,
whisper *Hide me*
I'd protect him with my life.
I chose this in my heart years ago,
never moved,
never changed my number.

眼鏡をかけたまま寝るのは
昔のままだ
時々呼吸がとまるのも
昔と同じだ
寝顔を見ていると
会わないでいた数年間が
液体のようなもので埋められていった

朝になってもその人は起きない
夜になっても、眠ったままだ
ひとを殺すとこんなにも
たっぷり眠れるものなのか
安らかな寝顔のその人はもう
息をするのさえやめたようなのだ

この日が来るのを待っていた
わたしがこの人の死に水を取る日
この日のために自殺もせず
車に轢かれてもくたばらなかった
冷たい飲み物をもう一杯作り
この人の口に少し含ませ
残りをわたしが飲みほした
もう何があってもきみをはなさないよ
古ぼけた映画のセリフみたいなことを思い
やせこけた頬をつついてみたりした

As always,
he slept with glasses on,
as always,
hiccupped in the night.
I watched his face sleeping
beneath the fluidity
of years.

Next morning, he had not awoken.
Evening, still asleep.
How can anyone sleep
so soundly
after killing?
His face was so peaceful, he'd even stopped breathing.

I'd been waiting for the day
when I'd offer his last rites.
For his sake, I never killed myself.
Even if I'd been hit by a car, I would not have died.
I poured one last glass,
wet his lips,
finished the rest myself.
I stroked the hollow of his cheek
like a line from an old movie:
Whatever happens, my darling, I'll never let you go.

七月七日

きょうもエアコンはいかれたままだ
ボタンを押すと白い煙が流れ
何かが焦げるにおいがする
ひと晩寝たら治るかと思ったが
そういうものではないらしい
電気屋に電話して修理を頼むと
ただいま大変混んでいますので
涼しくなるまでお待ち下さいといわれた

「ウソはいけませんよ、ヤマモトさん」
窓の下でまたあの男が電話している
「百八十万は無理でもね、十万二十マンコツコツと...」

そうだ、ウソはいけない
コツコツは大事だ
しかし一人二役に
そもそも無理があるのではないか
おととしの冬もエアコンは壊れた
暖かい空気が出てこなくなった
冷やすなら冷やす、暖めるなら暖める
どちらかひとつの役目なら
具合が悪くならずにすむのではないか

男一　　（ドンドンドン。ドアを叩いて）レイコさーん。
男二　　いるんでしょう、レイコさん。
ちょっと顔を見せてよ。

Is It July?

The window unit's been dead for a while now.
When I push the button, white smoke belches out.
It smells like something's burning.
I figured if I slept on it
the problem would go away
but it didn't.
I called the repair shop and they told me
We're extremely busy right now; you'll have to wait until the
weather cools down.

That guy beneath my window is on the phone again.
There's no need to lie, Mr. Yamamoto.
If you can't do the whole eighteen hundred, then what about one
or two hundred at a time, little by little . . .

That's right. Lying is bad.
Doing things little by little is what's important.
But how can one person
do both?
If you're gonna be a cooler, then cool; if you're gonna be a
heater, heat.
Two winters ago, the window unit broke;
warm air wouldn't come out.
If the unit had only one role,
I bet it would work without breaking.

OFFICER 1: (Banging on door) *Rei—ko?*
OFFICER 2: *You're in there, aren't you, Reiko?*

男一　　（ドンドンドン。ドアを叩いて）レイコさーん。
男二　　いるんでしょう、レイコさん。
ちょっと出てきなさいよ。

気温が三十一度をこえると
暑さで溶けてしまわないよう
人は話し声のボリュームをあげる
大きな声が五人分集まると
気温は三度上昇する

男一　　（ドンドンドン。ドアを叩いて）レイコさーん。
男二　　いるんでしょう、レイコさん。
さっきあんたの部屋から出てきた人が
頭から血を出しててさー。
　　ちょっと話を聞かせてよー。

一人一役のやり取りが
順調に続いて夕方になる
エレベーターの脇には
誰かが置いた七夕の笹が立ってかけてあり
「十万二十マンコツコツと」
「いるんでしょう、レイコさん。
ちょっと顔を見せてよ」
という短冊がぶら下がっている
暑苦しい字で
わたしも願い事を書く
「早くエアコンが治りますように」

Just come out for a second.
OFFICER 1: (Banging on door) *Rei—ko?*
OFFICER 2: *You're in there, aren't you, Reiko?*
Come out, we need to talk to you.

When it's over eighty-eight degrees,
people who haven't melted
raise their voices.
Five loud voices together,
the temperature goes up five degrees.

OFFICER 1: (Banging on door) *Rei—ko?*
OFFICER 2: *You're in there, aren't you, Reiko?*
A man bleeding from his head
just came out of your apartment.
Please, we need to know what happened.

The whole cast of characters continues to play their roles
into evening. In the foyer,
someone's arranged bamboo grass for the *Tanabata* holiday
where people write wishes for love
on strips of hanging paper.
One reads:
How about little by little, one or two thousand at a time.
Another: *Reiko, Come out,*
we need to talk to you.
I also write a wish for love:
Please, window unit, get well soon.

八月七日

小説を一本書き終えた
一七〇枚になってしまった
こんなに長くする必要はないのに
書いているうちにどんどんのびた
あしたは父の命日だ
生きていたら七十四歳
命日を前に書き上げることができたのは
父が力を貸してくれたからだろう
手帳を見ると去年のきょうも
小説を一本書き終えている（一五〇枚）
お父さんいつもありがとう
来年もよろしくね

引き続き二〇枚のものを書かなくてはならない
一七〇枚と二〇枚では書き方が違う
二〇枚の書き方がわたしには謎だ
誰かの力を借りたいけれど
しばらく誰の命日もない
一七〇枚から二〇枚ピンハネしてしまおうか
原橋はまだうちにある
あさって
新宿で編集者に会って
手渡すことになっている
二時に会う約束だが
もしかすると一時だったかもしれない
二時か　一時か
いったん迷い始めるとどこまでも迷い続けて

Is It August?

I finished writing this year's novel.
It came to 170 pages.
It didn't need to be that long, but as I was writing, it grew and
       grew.
Tomorrow is the anniversary of my father's death.
He'd be seventy-four.
Dad must've lent me strength
so I could get the novel written
before the anniversary of his death.
Looking through my notebook, this day last year,
I was just finishing writing a different novel (150 pages).
Thanks, Dad, as always,
for next year too.

My next gig is a twenty-pager.
The writing style is different for twenty pages than for 170
       pages,
twenty pages is a struggle for me.
I want to borrow someone's strength
but there are no other deaths coming up.
Could I skim twenty pages off the 170 pages
sitting at home?
I'm supposed to meet my editor
in Shinjuku, day after tomorrow.
We have a two P.M. appointment
or maybe it was one P.M.?
Two o'clock? One o'clock?

成仏できない
電話で確認すればすむ話だが
ばかだと思われそうでできない
あいだをとって一時半にいくことにしよう

一七〇枚と二〇枚のあいだに
五〇行の詩（＝これ）を書かなくてはならない
二〇枚のピンハネは無理でも
五〇行ならちょろいのではないか
一七〇万入った財布から
五〇円抜き取るようなものではないか
しかし紙幣から硬貨をどうやって抜き取る

「詩なのか」（詩七日）といいながら
お前のはただの詩ではないか
どこが「詩なのか」なのかと
知らない人が因縁をつけていた
すみません　たて棒を一本増やして
「詩なのだ」（詩七田）にしますといいながら
その人の腕をひっこ抜いてやった
抜いた腕を借りて三行書いた
父によく似た筆跡だった

I can't just call and confirm by phone
without looking like an idiot,
and once I get lost like this, there's no end
my spirit will never be able to rest,
so I decide to split the difference,
go at one thirty.

Along with the 170-page novel, and the twenty-page short
        story,
I also have to write this fifty-line poem.
Skimming twenty pages from myself for a short story turned
        out to be impossible,
but stealing fifty lines for a poem should be easy
as taking fifty cents
out of a wallet containing seventeen thousand dollars,
but you can't pull coins out of banknotes.

Is It Poetry?
sounds like the perfect title of a poem for my editor.
He might not understand, might pick a fight, saying
but in what way is "Is It Poetry?" poetry?
Also sorry, one more complication—
I call it *Yes, it is Poetry,*
pull out Dad's arm,
use it to write the remaining three lines
in his handwriting—

九月七日

きのうのうちにくればよかった
わたしは大きすぎる長靴を持っている
小さすぎる傘も持っている
土砂降りでも出掛けることはできたのに

きのうのうちにきていたら
東横線の急行で
おじいさんに席を譲ることはなかった
お礼にぶどうをいただいて
荷物をひとつ増やすこともなかった
きのうのうちにきていたら
画廊をひとり占めできたのに
声高に話すグループに
足を踏まれずにすんだのに

きのうのうちにきていたら
轢かれたカエルと目があうことはなかった
たまたま入った楽器屋で見た
親指ピアノがほしくなることもなかった
きのうのうちにきていたら
みなとみらいの観覧車に乗り
土砂降りを攪拌することもできたのに

ひとりがいやなら誰か誘えばよかった
晴れた日には台所でおろおろしている
雨友達が何人もいる
土砂降りの日なら喜んで
つきあってくれたはずなのに

Is It September?

I have everything necessary for a downpour:
the oversized boots, the too-small umbrella.
I wish I'd gone out yesterday
but I just stayed in.

If I'd gone out yesterday,
I would have given my seat
on the Toyoko Express to an old man,
would have been given grapes as gratitude,
one more bag to carry.
If I'd gone yesterday
to the art gallery, I'd have had the whole
place to myself, I wouldn't have gotten
my foot stepped on by a noisy crowd.

If I'd gone out yesterday,
I would have made eye contact with a run-over toad,
would have yearned for the thumb piano
in a music shop.
If I'd gone out yesterday,
I could have stirred the rain
on the Ferris wheel at Harbor of the Future park.

If being alone was part of the problem,
I could have invited someone else.
I have a ton of rainy-day friends.
On a sunny day, they stay home, flustered in their kitchens,
but when it pours, they're happy, glad to get together.

きのうのうちにきていたら
中華街で
まずい小籠包をほおばることはなかった
四十五分も待たされたあげく

雨あがりの土曜は尻軽女
前料待ちや所帯待ちや癇癪待ちに
おいでおいでと手招きをする

ゆうべのうちにあがったはずの雨は
夜になるとまた降り出した
肉まんを売っている店の隣で
あんこ入りの傘を一本買った
きのうのうちにきていたら
こんな変な傘は買わずにすんだのに

きのうのうちに横浜にくればよかった
何も予定はなかったのに
部屋で雨を見ていただけなのに
きのうのうちにこなかったのは
もちろん土砂降りのせいではない

If I'd gone out yesterday,
I would have waited forty-five minutes
in Chinatown
to fill my mouth with tasteless soup dumplings.

Saturday after rain is a loose woman
beckoning *Hey there!*
Soliciting tourism, families, tantrums.

When the rain that stopped
yesterday afternoon
started again in the evening,
I would have bought
a coconut-cake umbrella
by the pork bun shop.

Of course it's not the rain's fault
I didn't go to Yokohama yesterday.
I had no special plans,
just watching the rain
from my apartment.

十月七日

買う気もないのにオープンハウス
見に行くつもりになったのは
地下屋があると聞いたから
リバーサイド富士見町、一〇三号
フローリングの二つの部屋と
六帖ほどの小さな地下屋
地下屋には窓がないので
空気は多少すくなめです

最後の電車も出たあとだから
ふた駅分を川に沿って歩く
いつのまにか雨が降り
いつのまにかやんだらしく
街灯からこぼれたあかりが
路上でぱちぱちはねている

オープンハウス
開いているのは土曜と日曜
それも夕方六時まで
今はもう火曜だし
深夜だし
ドアは閉まっているだろう
だから安心して見に行ける
排気ガスがにおう京王バス車庫や
明るい人を募集する貼り紙の前を
かるがると通り過ぎ

Is It October?

Open House: Riverside Fujimi Town #103,
two rooms with wooden flooring
and a small finished basement.
A ninety-eight-square-foot basement
with no windows,
no circulation.
I'm not buying; I'm going
for that windowless basement.

It's well past the last train,
I walk the last two stations myself,
along the river, light spills from streetlamps
spattering the pavement.
Before I know it, it's raining.
Before I know it, it quits.

I slip past the Keio Bus Company's garage that smells like
       exhaust,
its bright HELP WANTED sign
seeking people for client-facing roles.
OPEN HOUSE
SATURDAYS, SUNDAYS
UNTIL 6 PM,
but it's Tuesday,
also midnight,
which is why I can go—
the door should be locked.

わたしは人に疎まれている
蔑まれてもいるらしい
でもそんなことどうでもいい
空気も光も足りない地下なら
人の陰口も届かない

やんだはずの雨がぽつぽつと
またぽつぽつと落ちてきた
小学校の金網に使い捨ての傘が三本
仲良く首を吊っている
一本もらおうと手を伸ばしたが
思い直して引っ込めた
雨にぬれながら歩く権利は
女にだってあるだろう

リバーサイド富士見町、一〇三号
窓にはシャッターがおりている
「即入居可」の　「築五年」
「新規内装手入れ済み」
インターホンを押しても
もちろん返事はかえってこない
前に住んでいた人はさらに深くもぐり
地下室のしたの地下室で
耳をふさいで眠っているから

I'm alienated by people.
I can feel their contempt.
But that's OK.
In an underground room with no air, no light,
insults don't bother me.

Pitter patter rain that had stopped
starts falling, *pitter patter*.
Three discarded umbrellas
hang by their necks
from an elementary school's chain-link fence.
I reach my arm out, think about taking one,
change my mind, draw it back again.
A woman has the right to get wet walking in the rain.

Riverside Fujimi Town #103
Shutters closed.
AVAILABLE FOR IMMEDIATE OCCUPANCY   NEWLY REMODELED
          INTERIORS
NEWER BUILDING (5 YEARS)
Of course no one replies
when I try the intercom.
The person who lived there before must have dived down
into the underground room below the basement,
asleep, hands over her ears.

十一月七日

マルコに耳を切られた
いつか切られるだろうという予感はあったが
まさかきょうだとは思わなかった
耳みとじゅっと音がして
熱いものがぽたぽた首すじを落ちる
マルコはあわててティッシュで傷口をおさえる
力をこめるから余計に血が出る
マルコは床から耳を拾い上げ
どうもすみませんと頭を下げる
夕方のハサミはすべりやすくて
気にしなくてもいいよ　マルコ
耳も長く伸びたから
カットしようと思っていたこと

イズミ美容室は七階にある
まわりに高い建物はないし
南に向かいて大きな窓が広がっているので
いつでも空が丸見えだ
月に一度エレベーターで空を見にきて
ついでに髪を短くしてもらう
下界は雨でも七階までくると
空は毎日晴れている
高いところで空を見ると
気持ちがいいのはなぜだろうと
ここにくるたびに考える

Is It November?

I had a hunch St. Mark
would cut off my ear, but no way
did I think it would be today.
My ear went *swoosh*,
hot stuff drizzling down my neck, St. Mark pressing
tissues against the wound with such force
extra blood came out.
St. Mark scooped the ear up off the floor, bowed his head,
said *I'm so sorry.*
Don't worry about it, Mark. Scissors
tend to slip at the end of the day
besides, my ears were so long, I was thinking
about getting them cut anyway.

From the wide, south-facing windows
of the Izumi Salon on the 7th Floor,
the entire sky is always available,
no other tall buildings.
I take the elevator once a month
to see that sky while getting my hair shortened.
Even when it's raining in the world below,
on the 7th Floor the sun shines every day.
Whenever I come, I always wonder why
watching the sky from high places
makes me feel so good.

マルコは丸子　尾道の人だ
俺が高校のとき大林監督が
映画の撮影に尾道にきたっすよ
そのころ俺バンドやってて
髪をトサカにするのが一番うまくて
あ、俺、将来美容師になろうと思って
専門学校にいったんすよ
キリストが磔にされたとき
ヘアメイクしたの俺っすよ
そういうとマルコは
窓からひょいと
わたしの耳を投げ捨てた

マタイ、マルコ、ルカ、ヨハネ
キリストの弟子たちがいる美容室
片耳を失うぐらいの受難は覚悟の上だ
マタイ、マルコ、ルカ、ヨハネ
片耳がなくても空は見える
両耳そろっているよりむしろ
空の広さを実感できる
空には耳
無数の空耳
そのうちのいくつかが
迷える羊雲になることも
耳をなくして初めてわかる

St. Mark's real name is Maruko.
She's from Onomichi.
Back in high school, the famous director—
you know, Obayashi?—shot a film in Onomichi.
Round that time, I was in a band,
was number one at hair gel.
Thought I'd do hair in the future.
Even went to hair school—
When Christ went up on the cross,
I was the one who did his hair and makeup, Maruko said
as she tossed my ear
out the window.

Matthew, Mark, Luke, John
A hair salon with Christ's disciples.
Matthew, Mark, Luke, John.
More than enough to handle the Passion of losing an ear.
At least it's just one ear, at least I have the sky.
Even with one ear,
I can still see and feel the sky's breadth
better than with both ears.
Now for the first time I understand
countless ears across the sky,
some wandering, a lost flock
of clouds.

十二月七日

久しぶりに神保町を歩けば
ある古本屋の店先に
「インコをさがしています」の貼り紙
「十一月二十三日の朝いなくなりました
名前はチーちゃん
見つけてくれた方には謝礼を進呈します」

いなくなってから二週間が過ぎている
生きていないだろうとに咄嗟思った
飢え死にするか　凍死するか
他の生き物の餌食になるか

インコはもともと熱帯の鳥だ
日本にいるのがそもそもおかしい
インコはインコの国に帰ればいいのだ
無事に帰ったチイーちゃんを見て
家族は泣いて喜ぶだろう
チイーちゃんと呼ばれて監禁されていたことを
チイーちゃんはマスコミに語るだろう

神保町をさらに歩けば
今度は「子猫あげます」の貼り紙
いなくなったインコのかわりに
小さな猫を飼うのはどうか
チーちゃんと名付けて可愛がっていたら
そのうちインコになるかもしれない

46

Is It December?

I go back to Jinbōchō
and walk around,
see a poster in front of a used book store:
Lost Parrot "Chee"
Last seen morning of November twenty-third
Reward offered to anyone who finds her.

It's been more than two weeks since Chee disappeared.
She's probably not alive anymore.
Starved? Frozen?
Fallen prey?

Anyway, parrots are tropical birds
outlandish in Japan.
It'd be great for parrots to go back to their parrot countries:
Little Chee's parrot family would cry with joy
at her safe return.
Chee herself would speak to the media:
they locked me in a cage and forced me to go by the name Chee.

I keep walking around Jimbocho,
This time it's Free Kittens.
How about a little kitty
instead of a missing parrot?
If I named it Chee, and cherished it,
it might even turn into a parrot.

「インコをさがしています」
人に頼るな　貼り紙に頼るな
そんなに大事なものならば自分で空にさがしにゆけ
鳥のふりして飛び回るうち
いつかインコになるだろう
家に戻って鳥籠に入れば
人間になったチーちゃんが
あなたの世話をしてくれる

昔　ウサギを飼っている人の家で
「ウサギの寿命ってどれぐらい？」
「だいたい五年ぐらいかな」
「このウサギいくつ？」
「今年で三歳」
その場に居合わせた人たちが
頭のなかで計算するのがわかった
引き算は残酷　もっと残酷なのは
そんな質問をしたわたし

神保町で見かけた貼り紙
チーちゃんの写真は色あせて
悪い病気にかかったよう
いなくなったのは今年ではなく
何年か前の十一月なのだ
わたしは道ゆく人に訊く
「インコの寿命ってどれぐらい？」

LOST PARROT

Don't rely on people. Don't rely on posters.
If it's important to you, go out on your own,
fly around in the sky pretending to be a bird.
Pretty soon you'll become the parrot.
Fly home
get into your cage,
Chee will become human and take care of you.

Once, at the house of my friend who had a rabbit, I asked:
How long do rabbits live?
Around five years.
How old is yours?
Three years old this year.
They understood I was doing the math in my head.
Subtraction is cruel.
But asking the question,
even crueler.

Chee's photo in Jinbōchō
is faded,
like she's deathly ill.
I realize she didn't disappear last month,
but a November years ago.
I ask people on the street *How long*
do parrots live?

十三月七日

七十をいくつか過ぎた人のために
化粧品を買いに行く
シミとシワをきれいに隠してくれる
液体ファンデーションを

初めて会った頃
この人はまだ二十代だった
あまり幸せではない結婚をして
不機嫌な顔で
赤ん坊のおしめを替わっていた

三十代のこの人も
楽しそうには見えなかった
カタカタカタとミシンを踏んでは
わけのわからないものを作っていた

四十代のこの人は
娘の日記をこっそりよんで
娘にきた手紙を勝手に開けた
娘が幸せにならないよう呪いをかけた
呪いは実によく効いたので
娘は毎日頭痛で悩んだ

五十代のこの人を知らない
わたしは遠く家を出たから

Is It January Again?

I buy liquid foundation
for someone in her seventies.
Makeup
to hide wrinkles and spots.

We first met when
she was in her twenties,
unhappily married,
sullen-faced
changing her baby's diapers.

She wasn't any happier
in her thirties,
sewing machine
clacking out inconceivable things.

In her forties, she
secretly read her daughter's diary,
opened her daughter's letters without permission,
cast a curse on her daughter: *may you never be happy.*
The curse worked so well that the daughter
suffered headaches every day.

I didn't know this person in her fifties,
I had moved far away.

六十代のこの人も知らない
一度も帰らなかったから

二十数年ぶりに会ったこの人は
七十をいくつか過ぎていて
母等というより老人だった
自分の母が
老人になる日がくるとは思わなかったので
ちょっと驚いた

四十代になったわたしは
この人の書いた買い物メモを読み
この人宛の請求書を勝手に開けて
支払いをすませる
七十を過ぎたこの人のために
化粧品を買いに行く
四十代の頃のこの人を
まだ許してはいないのに

シメやシワをきれいに隠す
液体のファンデーション
わたしはそれで
自分のこころを
隠そうとしているのかもしれない

I didn't know this person in her sixties,
I never went back even once.

By the time I met this person twenty-something years later,
she was well into her seventies,
more old person than mom.
I was shaken.
I'd never expected the day
when Mom would be old.

Now, in my forties,
I read her shopping lists,
open her bills without permission
and pay them.
Though I haven't forgiven her
for what happened in her forties,
I'm still buying makeup for her
in her seventies.

Liquid foundation
meant for hiding wrinkles and spots
might just be me
trying to hide
my own feelings.

十四月七日

わたし平凡になりました
平凡な女になりました
いいえもともと平凡ですが
平凡ゆえに
平凡であることを認めたくなく
ほかの人と多少違いはしないかと
平凡にうぬぼれておりました
けれどもう逃げも隠れもいたしません
わたしは平凡
きょうから平凡
いいえ生まれつき平凡でした

平凡は楽しい
平凡は明るい
お正月には神社にいって
神様に願い事をすればよい
桜が咲けば人込みに出掛け
きれいきれいを連発する
夏になったら海にいってはしゃぎ
クリスマスにはわけもわからず
グラスをかちゃかちゃ鳴らすのだ

平凡な男と平凡な女の
平凡なセックス
平凡な男は平凡な紐で
平凡な女のからだを縛り
平凡なアイスクリームを
平凡な女の

Is It February Again?

I became conventional.
A conventional woman.
Indeed, I was always conventional,
but on account of my conventionality
I was so conventionally conceited
I couldn't realize I was conventional;
thought I was just slightly different from other people.
I will no longer run or hide
from being conventional.
Today, conventional.
Actually, I was born conventional.

Fun to be conventional
in a bright way.
Nice to go to the temple on New Year's Day,
pray to gods for things I want,
picnic with crowds when the cherry blossoms bloom
and say *beautiful, beautiful* over and over;
frolic on the beach in summer,
rattle glasses at Christmas
without knowing why.

Conventional sex
between a man and a woman.
Conventional man tying up conventional woman's
conventional body with conventional rope,
happily licking conventional ice cream off conventional woman's
     nipples.

平凡な乳首にぬって喜ぶ
平凡な男が平凡な女の
平凡な兄か父だとしても
それはそれで平凡
平凡すぎるぐらい平凡な平凡

平凡なことに
平凡な人は平凡な病気にかかる
平凡な人にはそれが残念
何万人に一人の難しい病気に
平凡な人はあこがれる
平凡な病気に効く薬はたくさんあるから
平凡な人は平凡に回復し
平凡な社会に平凡に戻る

好きな人には優しくて
嫌いな人には意地悪をする
平凡な人の単純明快
悲劇を見て泣き
喜劇を見て笑う
平凡な人のあたたかさ
起きて動き　食べて寝る
平凡な一日
平凡な生涯
わたしはどこまで平凡になれるか

Even if, by convention,
he's her older brother or her father,
even that would be completely conventional.
So conventional,
it's unconventional.

Conventionally speaking,
conventional people get conventional illnesses.
That's unfortunate for conventional people.
Conventional people long for the
one-in-a-million disease.
There are tons of cures for conventional illnesses,
they recover in a conventional way,
return, conventionally, to conventional society.

I'm kind to the people I like,
mean to the people I don't like:
Conventionality, plain and simple.
I cry at tragedies,
laugh at comedies.
I'm warm.
I wake up   I eat and sleep
conventional days,
a conventional lifetime.
How much more conventional can I be?

十五月七日

雨が降っているらしい
推量の形を使うのは
見たわけではなく
それらしい音を
窓越しに聞いているからだ

「ダイアン、ここに銃がある。
これでウサギを撃ってこい」
ラジオで誰かが会話している
「ジョー、無理よ。そんなことできないわ」
「いいか、ダイアン。この小屋にはもう
クラッカー一枚のこっちゃいない。
飢え死にしたくなければウサギを撃つんだ」
「町にいって食べ物を買ってくるわ」
「片道だけで三日はかかる」
「平気よ。ついでに医師に寄って
あなたの傷に効く薬をもらってくるわ」
「そんなことをしてみろ。すぐ警察に通報されるぞ」

男がキツネと間違えて
犬を射殺したという記事を先月新聞で読んだ
殺されたのが犬　それも飼い犬だったから
犬も飼い主も気の毒に思った
おかしなことだが飼っていたのが別の動物
たとえばヘビかイノシシだったら
違う感想を抱いただろう
まして野生の生き物なら

Is It March Again?

I feel like it's raining.
The way I guessed
was not by looking,
but because of the rain-like sound
against the window

On the radio, two people are having a conversation.
You take this rifle, Diane, and go shoot us a rabbit.
I ain't got the gumption, Joe. I just can't!
Listen up, Diane: there ain't
  a cracker left in this cabin. If you can't
  get us a rabbit, we're done for.
I can go to town. Get us some provisions.
But we're three days outta town!
It'd be all right. I'll go to the doctor, get
  medicine for your wound.
You go right ahead then...get us
  reported to the police while you're at it!

In yesterday's paper,
a man shot a dog, thinking it was a fox.
The dog was killed—
someone's dog. It must have been terrible
for the dog and the owner.
Strange to say, but if it had been
a wild animal, a snake, a boar,
it would have hit me differently.

ダイアンが戻ってきた
「ああ、ジョー。どうしたらいいかしら」
「どうした。何があったんだ」
「ウサギを撃ったわ。あなたにいわれた通り」
「そうか。よくやった」
「でもそのウサギ、飼い主がいたの。
その人かんかんに怒って追かけてきたわ。
もうすぐここにくるはずよ」
「心配するな。そいつも撃ち殺してしまえばいい」

ラジオの受信状態が悪い
テレビをつけると同じドラマをやっている
「ああ、ジョー。どうしたらいいかしら」
「どうした。キツネと間違えて飼い犬を撃ったか」
「いいえ、ウサギを撃った猟師を殺してウサギの肉を奪ってきたの。
ウサギを撃つのはかわいそうだったから」
「心配するな。ウサギの敵を討ったと思えばいい」

窓の外でたえまなく降りしきる何か
雨のようだが　窓を開けると
銃弾かウサギに早変わりするかもしれない
目にするものと耳にするもの
どちらかひとつは正しいといえるだろうか

Diane came back:
Heavens, Joe. I just don't know what to do!
Now you tell me what happened.
I shot a rabbit. Just like you said.
How 'bout that now.
That poor rabbit had an owner. He got oh so
  angry and chased me. He's
  a comin' any moment!
S'all right, s'all right, just shoot the bastard.

Radio's got lousy reception, so I
turn on the TV and it's the same show.
Heavens, Joe. I just don't know what to do!
Now didn't you just shoot someone's dog, thinkin' it for a fox?
It wasn't that at all! I shot a hunter, took the rabbit he killed. I
      could never kill
      a poor little bunny.
S'all right, s'all right. Just tell yourself you saved all the rabbits
      from getting shot by him!

Something keeps pouring down outside my window
Sounds like rain   If I go to the window,
it could easily turn into bullets or rabbits.
Which one is right?
Should I go with my eyes or my ears?

十六月七日

姉がジャムを贈ったと聞いたので
妹はパンをプレゼントした
二人はとても仲がよかった

姉がロウソクを贈ったと聞いたので
妹は停電をプレゼントした
二人はとても仲がよかった

姉がまな板を贈ったと聞いたので
妹は鯉をプレゼントした
二人はとても仲がよかった

贈り先はすべて姉妹の母親
しとやかで上品なおばあさん
姉妹の父は数年前に他界した

姉が別荘を贈ったと聞いたので
妹はヨットをプレゼントした
二人はとても仲がよかった

姉が南極に招待したと聞いたので
妹はジャングルにつれていった
二人はとても仲がよかった

Is It April Again?

When she heard Big Sister had sent a jar of jam,
Little Sister sent bread.
The two of them were always in accord.

When she heard Big Sister had sent candles,
Little Sister sent a blackout.
The two of them were always in accord.

When she heard Big Sister had sent a butcher block,
Little Sister sent carp.
The two of them were always in accord.

Their mother was the recipient
graceful, elegant.
The sisters' father had left this world many years ago.

When she heard Big Sister had bought mother a summer house,
Little Sister bought mother a yacht.
The two of them were always in accord.

When she heard Big Sister had cordially invited their mother to
        Antarctica,
Little Sister enticed her to the jungle.
The two of them were always in accord.

ある日　母の姪
姉妹のいとこが
遠い国からやってきた
母はたいそう喜んだ
姉妹もたいそう喜んだ

姉が小島を贈ったと聞いたので
妹は猫をプレゼントした
それを聞いたいことは
ハツカネズミを贈った
三人はとても仲がよかった

いとこが太陽を贈ったと聞いたので
姉は日傘をプレゼントした
それを聞いた姉は
雨雲を贈った
三人はとても仲がよかった

ある日　母親が亡くなった
あるはずの遺産はどこにもなかった
姉はわめき
妹は寝込み
いとこはもう一人の伯母のもとに去った
三人はそれきり会うことはなかった
三人はとても仲がよかった

One day   the mother's niece,
cousin to the sisters,
joined in from a faraway land.
Mother was overjoyed.
The sisters, too, were overjoyed.

When she heard Big Sister had sent a small island,
Little Sister sent a cat.
When Cousin heard the news,
she sent fieldmice.
The three of them, always in accord.

When she heard Big Sister had sent the sun,
Little Sister sent a parasol.
When Cousin heard the news,
she sent a raincloud.
The three of them, always in accord.

One day   The mother died,
and left them nothing.
Big Sister wept.
Little Sister took to bed.
Cousin went off to another aunt.
The three of them, always in accord.
The three of them, never to meet again.

十七月七日

夕方六時になりました
風の強い日は時間のたつのが早い
時計の針が風にせかされるせいだ
公園では　　　おじいさんが
自転車に乗る練習をしている
風にあおられ　こけてばかりいるので
こける練習をしているみたいだ

ひとつき前
この公園で惨劇があった
それほど強い風でもないのに
しきりに桜が散ったのだ
花を散らすのは風の殺意
それとも枝の裏切りだろうか
地面を埋めつくした無残な死体は
もう一枚も残っていない
何も事件などなかったように

赤い雀の詩を読んで以来
そとを歩くたびに赤い雀をさがしてしまう
こんなに風の強い日は
どこからか降ってくると思ったが
白や黄色の雀ばかりが離着陸を繰り返す
赤い雀など最初から
詩のなかにしかいないのだろうか

Is It May Again?

Time flies on windy days
wind rushing clock hands.
Six in the evening
in the park   an old man
practices bicycling.
He's buffeted   all wobble
like he's learning how to wobble.

Tragic scene in this park last month—
cherry blossoms scattered
by wind less strong than today's.
What happened?
Was the weather murderous
or did branches betray their blossoms?
Of the pathetic corpses that once covered the ground,
not one petal remains.
Gone, like nothing ever happened.

Ever since I read the poem called "The Red Sparrow,"
when I go walking
I end up looking for red sparrows.
Where will they swoop down from
on such a blustery day?
White and yellow sparrows taking off, landing.
Do red sparrows exist only in that poem?

夕方六時になりました
六時になっても
おじいさんはまだこけてばかりだ
自転車が大きすぎるのだ
孫のおふるなのだろう
おじいさんの足は　みぎひだり
色の違う靴下をはいている
あれも孫のおふるだろうか
こけてばかりいるのは靴下のせいだ

わずかな風にも花は散るのに
強い風でも葉っぱは平気だ
葉っぱと風との間には
協定が結ばれているらしい
自転車の車輪も　雀の羽根も
おじいさんの小さな目鼻も
今にも吹き飛ばされそうなのに

ずっとおじいさんを見ているうちに
古い知り合いのような気がしてきた
もっと見ていると
おじいさんの靴下が赤い雀に見えてきた
さらに見ていると
このおじいさんこそ赤い雀の詩を書いた
詩人そのひとに見えてきた

Six in the evening.
Even past six,
the old man still wobbling
on a bike that must have been a hand-me-down
from his grandkids,
wobbling because it's too big for him
mismatched hand-me-down socks
left foot   right foot
from his grandkids.

It seems that
leaves and wind
have reached an accord
bicycle wheels   sparrow feathers
the old man's facial features
could scatter at any moment.
Cherry blossoms scatter with a puff.

I start to feel like he could be someone I know.
I look more closely.
Is this the very poet
who wrote "The Red Sparrow?"
I look *even more closely*
and his socks begin to resemble
red sparrows.

十八月七日

しかしどうしてホトトギスだけ
特別扱いなのだろう
時鳥　子規　不如帰はもちろん
杜鵑　杜宇　蜀魂　沓手鳥
すべてホトトギスと読むらしいのだ
あんなに大きく美しい鶴も
あんなに鋭い目をした鷲も
一種類の漢字しか与えられていないのに
ほかの鳥の巣に卵を産みつけることの厚かましい鳥だけが
何種類もの書き方を有する
これも厚かましさゆえなのか
鰻丼と書いても
火縄銃と書いても
ホトトギスと読むのかもしれない

テッペンカケタカ
もしくは特許許可局と
ホトトギスは鳴くといわれる
ホトトギスの声をいくら聞いても
テッペンカケタカとはどうしても聞こえない
「テッペン」は「ペン」にアクセントがあるが
ホトトギスは「テッ」の部分に力を入れて鳴いている
おかしい　もしかすると別の鳥の声と
間違えて伝えられたのではないか

調べていくと
天辺カケタカと鳴く　と書かれた歳時記があった

Is It June Again?

What's up with the cuckoo bird?
Why so many allusions?
A voice, a mystery.   *wandering Voice*   *darling of the Spring!*
Everyone knows the basics but there's also:
Cuckoo, cuckoo!—O word of fear
The majestic, beautiful crane
the sharp-eyed eagle
still only have one official name
while the cuckoo,
brazenly laying its eggs in the nests of other birds
has countless allusions.
Maybe it's the brazenness.
Even *pizza* or *pirate sword*
could be cuckoo references.

Someone told me the cuckoo's call
is either *ka-ka-ka-ka-kow-kow*
or *Farewell Farewell Poppinjay*.
When I hear the cuckoo, I can barely
hear *Farewell Farewell Poppinjay*;
the stress is supposed to be on the *Fare*
but the cuckoo puts the punch on *Poppin*.
It's weird—maybe they've confused the call
with the voice of a different bird.

It turns out *Farewell Farewell Poppinjay*
is from a dictionary of poetic references.

特許許可局という要領でテンペンカケタカと発音すると
（つまりテンとケタを強くいうと）
ホトトギスの鳴き方に似てなくもない
天辺とは「空の高いところ。空のはて」（広辞苑）
天辺が欠けるのは　フロンガスが原因で
オゾンホールができることをいう
のだろうか

早朝五時
神田川にかかる小橋を渡る時
ネッシーをうんと小さくしたような黒い生き物が
水中に沈むのが遠目に見えた
何だろう　今のは何だったのだろう
生き物が消えあたりに近づいて
ふたたび浮いてくるのを待って
やがて現れたその生き物は
カーブした長い首と
長いクチバシをもっていた
鵜だよ　これは鵜であるよ
名前の最初の一音が
最後の一音でもある母音の水鳥
この川で鴨や鷺は時々見かけるが
鵜を目にするのは始めてだ
潜るのが得意なその黒い鳥は
たびたび水中に姿を消しては
ほかの母音を探すのだった

If you pronounce *Farewell Farewell Poppinjay*
like *ka-ka-ka-ka-kow-kow*
(changing *Farewell* to *Farther,* and stressing *Pop*)
then you're not too far from the way the cuckoo actually sings.
Farther: "Beyond the sky."(Kōjien Dictionary)
The sky has problems like a hole in the ozone layer;
freon gas.

At five in the morning,
while crossing the Kanda River on a small bridge
I see a black creature in the water,
like a shrunken Loch Ness Monster sinking.
What on earth?
I wait for the creature to resurface
at the spot where it disappeared.
It soon appears, long
curved neck, long beak.
My first time seeing a cormorant
on this river; usually it's ducks and herons.
Of course: a cormorant. Cormorant.
c-*OR*-m-*OR*-ant,
a water bird with *or*
twice in its name.
The *or* bird that's good at diving
often disappears underwater
seeking other conjunctions.

十九月七日

わたしが夜通し起きていることを知っている人が
電話してきて
あたし大事な用があるから
七時にモーニングコールしてくれという
おやすい御用と請け負ったけれど
絶対寝てはいけないと思うと
とたんにまぶたが重くなる
いつもはたちまち過ぎる時間が
今夜はじっととまったままだ
朝まで起きている自信がないので
誰かに電話し
あした大事な用があるから
七時五分前にモーニングコールしてくれるよう頼もうとしたが
おやすい御用を請け負ったその人は
とたんにまぶたが重くなり
別の誰かに電話して
あした
七時十分前にモーニングコールしてくれるよう
頼むことになるかもしれない
こういうことを悪循環というのか
循環バスはあすも順調に
循環器糸統を走るだろうか（つまらんシャレだ）

　どうせ友人を起こすなら
歌をうたって起こしてあげよう
モーニング（ソング）コールというわけ
「愛唱名歌集」をぱらぱらめくると

Is It July Again?

I get a phone call from a friend.
She wants me to wake her up at seven A.M.,
because she knows I don't sleep.
It's for something important, she said.
Seems simple enough,
but as soon as I tell myself
just don't fall asleep
my eyelids droop.
The hours that always seem to disappear
have come to a dead stop tonight.
I have a feeling I won't be able to stay up until morning,
so I call a different friend:
I've got something important tomorrow
so could you wake me at six fifty-five A.M.?
She likely felt her eyelids droop, too,
called someone else,
Can you wake me up tomorrow at six fifty A.M.?
A vicious cycle
making its rounds
like a circulator bus
through my circulatory system
(how boring!)

I want the wake-up call for my friend
to be a song, sort of a "Morning Call."
Flipping through the pages of *Beloved Musical Classics*:
Mozart's "Lullaby"
Brahms's "Lullaby"
Schubert's "Lullaby"

「モーツァルトの子守歌」
「ブラームスの子守歌」
「シューベルトの子守歌」と
眠気をもよおす歌ばかり並んでいる
その罠を何とかかいくぐると
突然「ほととぎす」が現れた
一ヶ月ぶりの
ほととぎすとの再会
今度のほととぎすは
近藤朔風訳詞、ライトン作曲の
明治の歌だ

わたしはこの歌を知っている
高校の音楽の授業のとき
松山先生はピアノでこの曲を弾いたが
生徒に一度歌わせただけで
はい、次といって
「サンタルチア」に移ってしまわれた
「ほととぎす」は教育上
あまり重要ではなかったらしい
（いい歌なのに）
昔　歌いそこなったぶんを取り戻そうと
わたしは繰り返し
繰り返し「ほととぎす」を歌う
朝の七時はとうに過ぎたが
それでも歌をやめることができない

music that only puts you to sleep,
a trap sprung open when "The Cuckoo Bird Song"
suddenly appears.
It's been a month since my last encounter
with a cuckoo bird.
This time, the cuckoo
is a song by W. T. Wrighton, translated
into Japanese by Sakuto Kondo
in the early 1900s.

I know this song
from high school music class,
Miss Matsuyama played it on the piano.
We were allowed to sing it only once
before she moved us right along
to "Santa Lucia."
I guess "The Cuckoo Bird Song"
didn't have great educational value
(although it's a good song)
I sing "The Cuckoo Bird Song" over
and over,
trying to recall the parts I got wrong   in high school
It's well past seven in the morning
and I still can't stop singing.

二十月七日

何年も
友人に借りたままの本のなかに
漂母という言葉を見つけた
何度か
繰り返して読んだ本なのに
今まで漂母を見過ごしていた

漂母って何だろう
家出し　漂泊する母親だろうか
海で溺れる母親だろうか
辞書を引くと
「洗濯をする老婆」とあった
予想したより常識的な母の姿だった

この場合の洗濯とは
「綿や布を水でさらすこと」
洗剤も洗濯機も使わないらしい
川に洗濯にいき
桃を拾ったおばあさん
ああいう人が漂母だろう
漂母はとってもエコロジカル
そのご褒美に桃太郎をさずかった

漂母は今でもいるのだろうか
きのう見かけたおばあさんは
犬をつれて歩いていた
おばあさんが着ている服は

Is It August Again?

There was this word, *biddy*,
in a book I borrowed from a friend
years ago.
I had always overlooked *biddy*
even though I'd read the book
countless times.

What is a *biddy*?
Someone who bids   on horses?
An itty-bitty person?
According to the dictionary,
a more matronly, common-sense definition than I'd expected:
"an old maid who does laundry."

In those days, *laundry* meant
rinsing cloth and cotton in water:
no machine, no suds.
Imagine the biddy from the Peach Boy fairytale
picking peaches
on her way back from the river,
discovering the mythical Peach Boy
as a reward for her eco-friendly lifestyle.

Are there any biddies alive today?
 It could have been the old lady I passed yesterday
but her clothes smelled like laundry detergent,
which disqualified her.

洗いたてのにおいがした
犬はからだを洗われるのが
あまり好きではなさそうだった

きょう見かけたおばあさんは
小さな孫をつれて歩いていた
洗っても洗っても
孫はすぐに服を汚してしまう
汚れた服を脱がすとき
おばあさんは一瞬
快感を味わうのだった

おととい見かけたおばあさんは
自分の影をつれて歩いていた
洗濯に失敗し
ところどころ縮んでいる影だった

漂母は今や
辞書のなかにしかいないのかもしれない
古い辞書のなかで
毎日洗濯ばかりしているのかもしれない
洗うものもとうになくなって
自分の目玉や入れ歯をはずしては
しきりに水にさらしている漂母

Also, the dog she was walking
didn't look like it would enjoy
being washed.

Today's biddy, also no biddy.
Her grandson's clothes, instantly dirty,
no matter how much she washes.
She loves too much
the long moment
when she helps the little boy take off
his dirty clothes.

As for the lady I saw two days ago
she was no biddy either,
walking her shadow, which was shrunk in places
where she didn't wash it right.

At this point, biddy
only exists in an old dictionary.
Nothing left to wash except
her glass eyeball,
her dentures.
Just washing all day
in an old dictionary.

二十一月七日

西荻窪に　知り合いのライブを聞きにいく
その知り合い（Aさん）は会社を辞めて
もうすぐ関西に引っ越すという
なぜ引っ越すのかわたしにはわからない
Aさんにだってわからないのかもしれない

Aさんは普段ネクタイをしめて
地味なメガネをかけている
きょうはどちらもはずして派手なTシャツだ
Aさんに昼の顔と夜の顔があることを初めて知った
開け方や夕方の顔もあるのだろうか
二本のギターをかわるがわる抱え
マイクにむかって声をはりあげるAさん
知ってる人の知らない姿に照れて
ジンジャーエールを黙って吸った

十三年前　関西から出てきたわたしが
最初に住んだのが西荻窪だった
駅から徒歩十五分の古いアパート
歩けば歩くほど道はのび
なかなか部屋までたどりつけなかった
大家さんはきれいで品のいい老婦人で
関西にはいないタイプの人だった
月末に家賃を届けるたびに
じぶんが東京にいることを実感した

Is It September Again?

A friend of mine (let's call him Mr. X)
is performing live at a bar near Nishi-Ogikubo Station.
He has quit his job, will soon be moving to Osaka.
I don't know why he's moving away.
He himself might not know.

Usually, Mr. X wears a drab necktie
and glasses.
But today, he's wearing a flashy T-shirt.
Who knew Mr. X had a day look and a night look?
Does he have a dawn look and a dusk look?
He hollers into the mic
alternating between two guitars as he plays.
I chain-smoke ginger ale in silence,
feeling awkward, as I thought I'd known him.

Thirteen years ago,
I moved from Osaka   to Tokyo.
Back then, Nishi-Ogikubo was my station,
and my apartment, a fifteen-minute walk.
The more I walked, the longer the road seemed to get.
My landlady was an elegant, sophisticated older woman.
Each month, when I handed over my rent,
she gave me the sense that I was really,
truly living in Tokyo.

平日の午後　部屋にいると
玄関のカギが外からはずされ
ドアをあけて大家さんが入ってきた
わたしに気づくと「あら、いらしたの」と
平然といって出ていた
関西にいたとき　大家さんが
勝手に部屋に入ってきたことはなかった
やはり関西にはいないタイプの人なのだ

大家さんは何のためにわたしの部屋にきたのだろう
大家さんにもわからないかもしれない
わたしは何のために東京にきたのだろう
大家さんなら知っているかもしれない

ライブのあと
神明通りの信愛書店にいくと
大きなマンションに建ちかわり
その一階に移っていた
西荻窪にきた記念に本を買おうと思い
「正方眼蔵」を探したが
見当たらないので
「「奇譚クラブ」の人々」にした
どちらも似たようなものだろう
昼の顔と夜の顔が
道元にだってあっただろう

When I was in that apartment   on weekday afternoons
I'd hear someone turn the key in the entryway lock.
The door would open,
my landlady would step in.
Pardon me, she'd say,
I didn't know you were home, then leave.
My Osaka landlord would have never
come into my apartment uninvited.

Did my landlady even know
what she came into my apartment for?
I hadn't known why I moved to Tokyo,
but maybe she did.

After Mr. X's show,
I thought I'd buy a book at True Love Books, on Shinmeidori
            Avenue
to commemorate my return to the old neighborhood.
It's on the first floor now,
since they turned that building into brand-new condos.
I look for a copy of *Treasures of the Dharma*
but can't find it.
I settle on *The Joy of Bondage*.
Aren't they close enough?
Isn't S&M
Buddhism's night look?

二十二月七日

きょうもまだ金木犀が匂っている

今月一日
窓を開けると
金木犀がいきなり匂った
前日まで何の気配もなかったのに
この日はどこにいっても
金木犀の匂いがついてまわった
金木犀解禁日だったのかもしれない

十三年前の秋
飼っていた猫が事故死した
金木犀がきつく匂う日だった
以来　金木犀の季節がくるたびにつらかった
なのに今年は
ああ、いい匂いだと素直に思った
これはどういうことだろう
わたしはあの子を忘れかけているのか
全身真っ白の猫だったから
白い袋を見てもあの子に見えた
白い枕を見てもあの子に見えた
白い猫をみると
これはあの子ではないと
自分にきっぱり言い聞かせた
その習慣も
少しずつゆるくなっている

Is It October Again?

I can still smell the sweet olive tree.

No warning signs a day earlier,
but when I opened the window
on the first of October,
I smelled sweet olive wherever I went.
It was like the trapped fragrance
was let loose, lifted,
swirled around me.

The day my cat got hit by a car
thirteen autumns ago
also smelled of sweet olive.
Since then   I get sad every year at the smell.
This year the smell was lovely.
Does this mean
I'm starting to forget her?
Her body, pure white—
each time I saw a white cat, I thought
Is that her?
I used to see her in every white bag.
I used to see her in every white pillow.
I had to force myself
to say *that's not my cat*,
but I'm not doing that so much
anymore.

恐山にいくと
骨をまいたように地面が白かった
金木犀のかわりに硫黄が匂う
高いところで透明な湯がわき
低いほうへちろちろ流れていく
湯が流れ去り　乾いたあとは
黄色いまだら模様ができている

山は静かで
巫子はひとりしかいなかった
廊下には
もう若くはない女が四人
横座りをして自分の番を持っている
ガラス戸の向こうの巫子の声は聞こえず
女たちも口を閉ざしている
わたしも黙って横座りをした

猫の霊もおろしてくれるだろうか
まだ生きている父親の霊を
おろしてもらった人もいるらしいから
たぶん問題ないだろう
おろした霊に姿を与え
つれて帰ることはできるだろうか
死んだ猫と
金木犀を眺めながら
ゆっくり話がしたいのだが

On Mount Fear,
the ground is white like scattered bones.
The smell is hot sulfur
springs trickling from summit
to ground,
dry ground mottled yellow,
water gone.

The shrine at Mount Fear is a quiet place,
only one oracle,
so there's a line in the shrine corridor.
Four women, no longer young,
wait their turn, sit sideways.
I join them, sideways and silent.
The oracle, inaudible
on the other side of the glass.

I hear some people are visited
by their fathers' living spirits.
If so, why not a dead cat?
Is she willing to take form?
To come back?
Could I take her home,
if only for us to catch up,
enjoy sweet olive
together.

二十三月七日

ブッダはいう、ただ独り歩めと
犀の角のようにただ独り歩めと
「一切の生きものに対して暴力を加えることなく、
一切の生きもののいずれをも悩ますことなく」
「犀の角のようにただ独り歩め」

ブッダさん、ブッダさん
わたしはゆうべ激しく人をなじりました
なじる必要は全然なかった
静かに話せばすむことなのに
高ぶる感情を抑えきれませんでした
ゆうべ人に投げつけたひどい言葉が
きょう自分に届き　涙しています

ブッダはまたいう
「交わりをした者には愛恋が生ずる。
愛恋にしたがってこの苦しみが起こる。
愛恋から患いの生ずることを観察して、
犀の角のようにただ独り歩め」

はい、その人と交わりました
今でも愛しく思っています
けれど人は人　おのれはおのれ
いくら欲しくても手に入れることはできません
そういうことへのいらだちが
別の理由にかこつけて
その人をなじらせたのかもしれません

Is It November Again?

Be the rhinoceros. Wander alone.
Wander alone Buddha says,
be the rhinoceros. Wander alone
without violence against any living thing.
without troubling any living thing.

Last night I went too far.
There was no reason to be so mean to my love.
Oh Buddha, Oh Buddha,
though I could have been more gentle,
I couldn't hold back boiling emotion.
The insult I hurled
came back to me today   as endless tears.

Buddha also says
In any given group of people, someone always falls in love.
They suffer this romance.
Be the rhinoceros. Wander alone
to see how love suffers.

That was me, alright. I fell in love.
I love them still.
But people are people, I am me.
The real reason I was so unkind
is anger
at never getting what I wish for
no matter how badly I want it.

ブッダはまたこうもいう
朋友・親友に憐れをかけ、
心がほだされると、おのが利を失う。
親しみにはこの恐れのあることを観察して、
犀の角のようにただ独り歩め」

これは少々冷たいお言葉
その人のためならおのが利を失うことも厭いません
その人の利のために
おのが利を捨ててもいいとさえ思っています
わたしが利というものを待ち合わせているとしてですが

ブッダはまだこういう
「実に欲望は色とりどりで甘美であり、
心に楽しく、種々のかたちで心を撹乱する。
欲望の対象にはこの患いのあることを見て、
犀の角のようにただ独り歩め」

はい、その人こそ欲望の対象　甘美のみなもと
つねに心は乱されます
対象から遠く離れて　犀の角のようにも
牛の角のようにも歩みたいと思うのですが
あまりに対象が愛しくて一歩も歩き出せないのです

「　」内は岩波文庫「ブッダのことば」（中村元訳）からの引用です。

Have mercy on your friends and loved ones,
Buddha continues,
when the heart is troubled, the heart loses its mind.
Be the rhinoceros. Wander alone,
knowing you've lost your mind.

Harsh words from the Buddha.
I don't mind losing my mind.
What good is it to have a mind?
I threw out my mind
for love's sake.

Buddha also says:
Desire's colors are delicious and sweet,
disturbing inner truth in many ways.
There is suffering in desire.
Be the rhinoceros. Wander alone

That was me all right, love,   the object of my desire
source of sweetness, source of suffering.
I don't want to be the rhinoceros,
wandering alone;   I'll be the cow, unable to wander
away from him.*

*   Translators' note: In a note originally included with this poem
in the Japanese edition, Hirata cites Moto Nakamura (1912-1999),
Japanese translator of *In Buddha's Words*, originally written in the
Pali language. We have translated Nakamura's Japanese texts into
English in the context of this poem.

二十四月七日

「この先、ゆれますのでご注意下さい」
のどかな声がバスのなかを泳ぐ
それは困ります、運転手さん
わたしは洗面器を抱えています
洗面器のなかには金魚が一匹
バスがゆれると水をひきつれて
金魚が飛び出してしまいます

「この先、ゆれますのでご注意下さい」
ゆらすのはあなた
それともバス自身ですか
風邪の予防には注射をします
ゆれを防ぐ注射はないのですか

実はわたくし乗り物に酔います
この先、吐きますのでご注意下さい
エチケット袋なんて持ってません
洗面器ならありますけど
金魚が泳いでいますから使うわけにはいきません
ゲロまみれの金魚なんて
あなた見たくないでしょう？

みちゆきって名前の知り合いが二人いました
ひとりは小学校の若い教師で
ひとりは高校の文芸部の先輩でした
親は何を考えてそんな名前をつけたのでしょうね
二人はその後道行きをしたかしら

Is It December Again?

A gentle voice swims through the bus:
Ladies and gentlemen: rough road up ahead. Please take care.
That will be a problem, driver.
I'm holding a plastic washbasin
with a goldfish in it,
The goldfish sloshes almost out of the water
at every bump.

Ladies and gentlemen, rough road up ahead. Please take care.
Driver, are you sloshing my goldfish on purpose,
or is the bus doing it on its own?
There are flu shots,
so can't there be an anti-sloshing shot?

Ladies and gentlemen, I'm about to throw up, please take care.
I'm prone to motion sickness.
No motion sickness bags on board.
I do have a washbasin
but there's a goldfish in it:
driver, do you really want
my goldfish covered in puke?

In my life, I've known two people named Journey.
(What parent in their right mind gives their child a name like
    that?)
One was a young teacher from elementary school;
the other, a fellow high school student in Literary Club.

たぶんしなかったと思いますよ
子どもはなかなか親の期待どおりには
いきませんもの

この金魚の名前もみちゆきっていうんですよ
ほら、口をぱくぱくさせて
何ていってるんでしょうね
死ぬか　死なぬか
死なぬか　死ぬか
わたしにはそう聞こえます
ええ、道行きをっ持ちかけられてるんです、わたし

「この先、ゆれますのでご注意下さい」
洗面器から金魚が飛び出し
バスの窓からわたしが飛び出す
それも道行きになるんでしょうか
全身打撲で
死ぬか　死なぬか
死なぬか　死ぬか
ずいぶん元気な道行きだあね

この先、ゆれませんのでご注意下さい
この先、死にますのでご注意下さい
この先、死にませんのでご注意下さい

Did they both go on journeys after that?
I'm guessing no.
Kids rarely live up
to their parents' expectations.

This goldfish is also kind of a *Journey*.
What could he be saying,
his little mouth opening and closing?
Will we die?   Will we survive?
Will we survive?   Will we die?
I feel he is proposing an adventure.
A journey?

Ladies and gentlemen, rough road up ahead, please take care.
The goldfish leaps from the washbasin,
I leap from the bus window
and so the journey begins,
a very lively jaunt
full of bruises:
Will we die?   Will we survive?
Will we survive?   Will we die?

Ladies and gentlemen, the rough stretch is ending, please take
        care.
Ladies and gentlemen, we should be experiencing some dying
        up ahead, please take care.
Ladies and gentlemen, we'll survive up ahead, please take care.

あとがき

この詩集は二〇〇二年２月号から〇四年１月号までの二年間、「現代詩手帖」に連載した作品をまとめたものです。ただし毎年一二月号は年鑑となり、連載はできないという同誌の性格上、「十一月七日」「二十三月七日」は未発表の書き下ろしです。

連載開始の少し前、もう詩はやめようと思っていた。自分の詩に飽き飽きしていたし、この先、詩とどう向き合えばいいかわからなくなってもいた。もちろんそんな気持ちになったのはこのときが初めてではない。詩との倦怠期はそれまでにも何十回となくやってきた。

旧知の編集者から連載の話を持ちかけられたとき、「もう詩はやめようと思っているんだよね」とわたしはいった。「やめてどうするんですか」「どうしようか。イナカに帰ってケッコンとするかな。豆腐屋か製材所の後妻がいいな」働き者のおかみさんに変貌した自分を思い描いてうっとりした。編集者は詩をやめることについて賛成も反対もしなかった。わたしが書かなくても代わりはいくらでもいる。自分はいてもいなくてもいい存在なのだとはっきり思い知らされた。

どうして連載を引き受ける気になったのかよく覚えていない。もしかすると、詩をやめることに反対してくれなかったからかもしれない。

連載第一回目、わたしは詩のあとにこう但し書きをつけた。

二〇〇二年一月より毎月七日を「詩を書く日」と決め、執筆にあて

Afterword and Notes

Toshiko Hirata

The poems in this collection were serialized in the Japanese literary journal *Notebook of Contemporary Poetry*, appearing monthly from February 2002 through January 2004. Because the December issue of *Notebook of Contemporary Poetry* is an annual review, however, the poems "Is It November?" and "Is It November Again?" are previously unpublished works.

Shortly before this serial publication began, I was actually thinking of giving up poetry. I was tired of my own work, and had no idea how to move forward. Of course, this was not my first time feeling this way: I had felt poetry fatigue many times before. When the editor, an old friend, asked me to write a series of poems for his journal, I told him "Actually, I've been thinking of giving up poetry." "What will you do if you give it up?" He asked me. "What to do indeed! Move back to the country and get married? Be the wife of a tofu maker or a sawmill operator?" I was captivated with the thought of myself transformed into a laborer. But my editor neither agreed nor argued with my plan to give up poetry. He said there are plenty of people who could write the series, making it clear that it truly did not matter if I showed up or not.

I don't know exactly why I decided to take on the series. Maybe it's because he didn't oppose my quitting poetry. Beginning in January of 2002, I declared I would write a poem on the seventh day of each month. The title of the series is pronounced *Shinanoka*, strictly meaning "Poems on the Seventh Day." However, *Shinanoka* also means "Is It Poetry?" So, in addition to referring to the task of writing a poem on the

ることにした。連載タイトルは「詩七日」。しなのか、と読む。七日
に書くという設定に加え、デビュー以来、「これが詩なのか」とい
われてきたことに由来する。

えらそうにいってみたものの、すらすらと書けるはずではない。終
日机に向かっても一行も浮かんでこないことがほとんどで実際に書
き上がるのは翌日、翌々日、翌々々日……。厳密にいえば「詩七
日」ではないのかもしれないが一篇仕上げるまではわたしにとっ
ては長い七日が続いているのだった。自分なりのルールとして、毎
月七日にあったことを詩のモチーフとした。つまり日記ならぬ月記
というわけ。

連載を始める前は、自分が書いているのは果たして「詩なの
か?」という疑問があった。今あらためて読み返してみると、よくも
悪くも詩でしかないという気がする。「詩なのか……(ため息)」と
いったところだ。それでは詩とは何かというと、それはよくわから
ないのだが。

詩人といえども生身であるから二年のうちには調子の悪いときもあ
る。いっそなかったことにしたい作品もまじっているけれど、ほか
のものと差し替えるのは卑怯である。多少の訂正は加えたが、連載
したものをそのまま載せることにした。

後半ホトトギスがやたらと出てくるのは、この時期、正岡子規に入
れあげていたからだ。「漂母」ということばも、子規の「漂母我を
あはれむ旅の余寒哉」という句で知った。「十七月七日」の「赤い
雀の詩を書いた詩人」とは小野十三郎のこと。「現代詩手帖」はこ
のとき関西の詩を特集していたので、わたしもこっそり自主参加し
たという次第。誰か気づいてくれただろうか。

seventh of each month, *Shinanoka* also anticipates the critical question: "Is what you wrote actually poetry?" (asked almost immediately after the series debut). I added the seventh day caveat to the series after publication of the first poem.

It's one thing to say you'll write a poem every month, but it was much harder to do it smoothly. Most months, I hadn't written so much as a single line by the seventh day. So it spilled into the next day, the day after that, the day after that, and so on. Strictly speaking, it wasn't so much a "poem on the seventh" as much as a long seventh day that stretched out for me until the poem was finished. As a rule, however, whatever I had on the page on the seventh became the theme of that month's poem.

Before the series debut, I also had to struggle with the question of whether or not I was actually writing poetry. When I look at it today, for better or for worse it does seem to be poetry, and with a sigh, I accept that it is. At this point, I'm not even sure what poetry is anymore.

As a poet and a living person, there were times during the two-year period when I wasn't up to writing a poem as scheduled. There are places where it would have been wiser to edit things out, but I felt it would have been dishonest to modify the text. With only minor corrections, I decided to publish the serialized version basically as-is.

「四月七日」には谷川俊太郎さんが登場する。「現代詩手帖」はこの号で谷川さんの特集を組んでおり、わたしはそちらに散文を書くことになっていた。谷川さんの本をまとめて読み、しばらく谷川漬けになっていたので詩にも谷川さんが出てきてしまった。できればほかのことを書きたかったが、うまく切り替えができなかった。詩を書くことは意外と生理的なことだと思った。谷川さん、無断で登場させてしまい、申し訳ございません。「八月七日」の小説はボツになりました。

平田俊子

Notes on Individual Poems

The reason the cuckoo bird appears in the second half of the book is because I was reading [Meiji-era haiku master] Shiki Masaoka at the time.

I also have Mr. Masaoka to thank for the word "biddy," which I discovered in his haiku "Biddy's Graceful Journey, Lingering Cold."

In "Is It May Again?" the "very poet who wrote *The Red Sparrow*" is Osaka-based poet Tōzaburō Ono [1903–1996]. That month, *Notebook of Contemporary Poetry* was featuring writers of Osaka so I snuck in the reference on purpose. I wonder if anybody noticed!

In "Is It April?" there are multiple references to the poet Shuntarō Tanikawa. That month, *Notebook of Contemporary Poetry* was featuring Mr. Tanikawa's work, and I was planning to write some prose for the journal as well. For this purpose, I read all of Tanikawa's books, and for a while I was so pickled in Tanikawa that he appeared in my own poetry. I wish I could have written something else, but I was unable to switch. Writing poetry during that period was surprisingly psychological. Mr. Tanikawa, I apologize for writing about you in this impermissible way.

The novel I mention in "Is It August?" was never completed.

Notes from the Translators

[Portions of this essay appeared in *Modern Poetry in Translation* (Spring, 2020), *Transference* (Fall, 2020), and *World Literature Today* (Fall, 2020).]

In real life, Toshiko Hirata (born 1955) is a uniquely kind, warm, and outgoing person, famous for her sense of humor as one of Japan's well-known living writers. In her award-winning collection *Is It Poetry?*, however, Hirata's choice of poetic speaker is a recluse: someone who struggles with the very idea of writing poetry, and for whom the noises of contemporary society are frequently too much to bear.

We chose to translate *Is It Poetry?* on the recommendation of Japanese poet Kiriu Minashita, whose award-winning book *Sonic Peace* we had translated already (Phoneme Media, 2017). At a 2018 meeting in Tokyo, Minashita provided Spencer Thurlow with a two-page list of contemporary Japanese poets she thought we might want to translate next. Spencer went straight from that meeting to the Kinokuniya bookstore in Shinjuku, and purchased as many books as he could find by the poets on the list.

We translated a number of sample poems, brought them to our team of readers, and together decided that Hirata's *Is It Poetry?* was the standout work that spoke to twenty-first-century American sensibilities. The poem that really sold us was "Is It June?" in which the situation is so dramatic (a murderer comes to stay the night) that it literally could not have been a true story. Yet Hirata tells the story so beautifully that it feels completely true.

We were also drawn to the fierceness of the project itself. An audacious task: writing a roughly 50-line poem on the seventh day of the month, each month, for two years. By asking the question herself ("Is It Poetry?") Hirata turned the entire endeavor into an ars poetica. The collection was a hit, and *Shinanoka* was awarded the Hagiwara Sakutarō Prize.

Hirata grew up on a very small island off the western coast of Japan. She earned her place in the contemporary canon as part of the "women's boom" in Japanese literature in the 1980s. In addition to being a poet, she's a prolific playwright and novelist, which explains her affinity for the dramatic. Hirata is a skilled dramatist who puts her beleaguered poetic speaker into seemingly-impossible situations. *Is It Poetry?* begins with her female speaker assuming a male frame of mind while riding the Tokyo subway and ends with her jumping out a bus window with a pet goldfish she's named Journey. The reader can take the entire book as a literary journey: a two-year sojourn through poetry.

The book's title is an intentional pun that posed an extraordinary challenge for us as translators. The Japanese title, *Shinanoka*, literally means "Poems on the Seventh Day." The original Japanese poems are titled in numeric sequence from "Month One Day Seven" through "Month Twenty-Four Day Seven." Crucially, the Japanese word *nanoka* means both "seventh day" and "is it?" and Hirata goes to great lengths to explain, in the poem "Is It August?" as well as in her Afterword, that the humorous wordplay is intentional. We decided, therefore, to call our American version "Is It Poetry?" and give up the meaning of "seventh day." Similarly, we decided to amplify Hirata's self-doubt by numbering the poems as questions: "Is It February?" (literally, "February Seventh" in Japanese) "Is It March?" etc. We went as far as to title poems thirteen through twenty-four (the second year of her project) "Is It January Again?" through "Is It December Again?" although the literal translations of the Japanese would have been "Month Thirteen Day Seven" through "Month Twenty-Four Day Seven."

In 2019, Spencer traveled to Tokyo and met with Hirata, who had already granted us permission to translate *Shinanoka*. She was happy with the humorous choices we'd made for her book title, poem titles, puns and wordplay, and she gave us clear permission to deviate from the Japanese as much as required. "Change whatever you need to," she said, "just keep it funny." We had no idea how difficult that would turn out to be.

Our Process

Just as we had done with Minashita's *Sonic Peace*, we used a workshop format to critique our translations of the twenty-four poems in *Shinanoka*. Our workshop consisted of two primary readers, Boston-area poets Grey Held and Alexis Ivy. Both Alexis and Grey had been part of our workshop for Minashita's *Sonic Peace*, and they knew that, since the sound of Japanese was going to be long gone from the final poem anyway, it no longer mattered what *words* we chose in English, only what *concepts* we got across. Alexis and Grey made sure we went out of our way to accommodate Hirata's American reader: they encouraged us to make significant changes in order to assure each American translation was just as experiential (and fun) as the Japanese-language original.

In addition to our workshop team, two other friends helped shepherd us through this project. Tokyo-based translator Miyuki Yokota Nōguchi was able to make sense of the more bizarre and fantastical situations in *Is It Poetry?*. For example, Miyuki (often, but not always) was able to clarify whether someone was alive or dead in a given poem, or whether something had or hadn't happened—troubling distinctions that were common throughout the book. Our friend Heather Nelson, an intersectionalist poet from Cambridge, MA, helped us read Hirata's work more closely from a feminist perspective. It was Heather who provided the crucial adjective, "conventional," that repeats thirty-two times in "Is It February Again?"

There is always a degree of learning required when introducing Japanese words into a translated poem in English. Our American reader will know what sushi is without the need for a Google search, but *Kansai* requires a bit more thought. Grey and Alexis rejected the word *Kansai*, and we replaced it with *Osaka* throughout the book—Osaka is the largest city in the Kansai region and is familiar to western readers as a Japanese place name. We believe that Hirata's primary purpose of writing poetry is for her reader's delight and astonishment, not for education. This understanding helped us notice that the appearance of Japanese words in our English-language translations was usually a subconscious effort on our part to cover up a deeper translation challenge. As a result, we made the conscious decision to use as little Japanese as possible.

It was hard, for example, to capture the lavish imagery in "Is It September" in a way that would appeal to readers holding no special knowledge of Japan. Grey and Alexis rejected "bean paste umbrella" (a type of pastry and our literal translation from the Japanese) because Western readers tend to think of beans as something savory. At that very moment the poem calls for something sweet, so we went with "coconut cake umbrella" instead. Our translated poems grew stronger the more we walked away from the urge to teach Japanese language and culture and focused, instead, on the touching strangeness of the situations Hirata creates.

Another good example of how we approached balance is how we came to the image "bear hug body pillow" in "Is It January?". In this case, the Japanese translates literally to "dog torso." Even before consulting our workshop team, we knew that the American reader would not understand "dog torso" no matter what we wrote around it. First of all, in English, the technical term would be "dog mannequin" for the object Hirata describes as a "torso," but even "dog mannequin" doesn't really conjure up an image, except maybe something you'd find in a pet shop. What is Hirata's concept then? It is a weird enough image already, so after some googling in Japanese, we found an eyeless stuffed animal that someone would sleep with for sale. Then we found a corresponding product in the U.S., the bear hug body pillow, that conjures up the proper imagery we believe Hirata wanted to communicate.

—*Eric E. Hyett and Spencer Thurlow*
Massachusetts, July 2020

Notes from the Translators
on Specific Poems

"Is It February?"

Noise complaints, and a general anxiety about the outdoors, are a recurring theme throughout *Is It Poetry?* Many of the poems feature a certain reclusiveness, which seems to have to do with noise and external stimuli causing distress. Hirata's poem begins with a complaint about "endless road construction."

In the second stanza, a crow nibbles off a *dakuten* (consonant change marker), which results in swapping the initial "V" in Vincent Van Gogh to an "F" sound: Fincent Fan Gogh. Literally, the crow must have eaten four strokes off the Japanese syllable *vu* and left the syllable *fu* in its place. At the end of the poem, the speaker once again complains about another consonant marker, a *handakuten* which creates the "soft p sound" in the word "polyp."

"Is It March?"

This theatrical poem is a wonderful example of how Hirata can isolate a scene and is also a demonstration of her literary breadth. We sometimes refer to Toshiko Hirata as a "playwright's poet," meaning she has an allegiance to dramatic narrative, and the poems in *Is It Poetry?* often follow a funny or tragic story arc that is narratively well-constructed.

Incidentally, Hirata told us that she actually wrote the play that is featured in this poem, but that it was never produced and is still sitting on a shelf somewhere.

"Is It October?"

In the poem "Is It October?" Hirata's speaker finds herself going far out of her way, in the middle of the night, to visit an empty condo listed for sale: "I'm not buying; I'm going / for that windowless basement." These lines encapsulate the bleakness of her speaker's outlook, as though the world's noise is too much to bear. Later in the same poem, however, Hirata allows her speaker some pleasure (as well as some autonomy) when she chooses to reject an umbrella: "A woman has the right to get wet walking in the rain."

In "Is It October?", the basement itself was problematic: we ran out of words to describe it in English (sub-basement? sub-sub-basement?), and it led to a conversation about whether she was deploying a metaphor for death. In the end, we decided the speaker is merely reclusive, not supernatural.

Finally, although the gender of the previous owner of the condo is unspecified in the Japanese poem, we chose to make her a woman, to best align with the alienated feelings of the speaker.

"Is It March Again?"

In "Is It March Again?" Hirata's speaker listens extensively to a radio drama that has a few different factors that point toward the genre being "American Western." We felt this was accurate because of the characters' names, Joe and Diane, and the fact they were both fugitives, hiding in a house three days from the nearest town.

But what kind of Western? The category itself is broad, and filled with iterations of fantasy. From this, we had to consider what the average Japanese audience would be expecting: if it were a Western, it would probably be the Hollywood 1960s era "spaghetti Western," or Hollywood's idea of what 1880s Arizona was like. The radio drama in Hirata's poem seemed quite domestic, however, and there were also police involved (as opposed to a sheriff or bounty hunter), so, while the "Wild West" or Sergio Leone might inspire the imagery, this was a little different. We finally decided to root through some popular Hollywood films of the '60s and '70s and settled on *Bonnie and Clyde*, which, after watching the film for reference (and stealing some dialogue) we felt best matched the tone of the radio dialogue in the poem.

Of course, *Bonnie and Clyde* is a 1960s Hollywood fiction based on the real-life bank-robber lovers in the 1920s American South—pretty far from what the American West was like in the 1880s. So, to sum it up, the dialogue in this poem is an interesting kind of simulacrum: a Japanese poet's fictional radio drama, inspired by 1960s Hollywood's idea of the 1920s American South, intended as a Western for a Japanese audience in 2003, and then translated back into American English in 2019. Is it poetry? We hope so.

"Is It June Again?"

In the poem "Is It June Again," Hirata interrogates the Japanese language itself, focusing on the fact that in Japanese, there are over thirteen ways to write the word "cuckoo" (to be specific, thirteen different *kanji* character compounds that all correspond to the same bird.)

This poem literally drove us cuckoo. Hirata's speaker consults a glossary of poetic references, as well as birdwatchers' guides, striving to connect meaning between them. The poem finishes with a complaint, echoed in the first lines, regarding the inequity among bird names: why does the *hototogisu*, or cuckoo, have many syllables and many *kanji* characters with which it can be written, while the cormorant (simply *u* in Japanese) has only one syllable and one associated character?

As you may have guessed, this presented numerous intractable problems for us as translators committed to not teaching Japanese to our readers. In our American version, we threw out the entire construct of *kanji* and focused on English literary references for cuckoo, replacing *kanji* compounds with allusions to Wordsworth and Shakespeare to fulfill Hirata's intent. We also replaced "vowels" in her poem with "conjunctions" in the American version, in order to make a joke about the cormorant that was actually funny.

It was a good thing we solved it here because, when the cuckoo bird appeared a month later in "Is It July Again?", we were ready for it.

"Is It November Again?"

This deeply moving poem is a departure from the rest of the book, and is one of only two poems in "Is It Poetry?" that were never serialized in print. About half the lines in the poem are direct quotations from a Japanese book called *budda no kotoba* (*In Buddha's Words*), a canonical early-Buddhist text originally written in the Pali language. This is the only poem in the book for which Hirata adds a note at the bottom of the poem: she acknowledges Moto Nakamura (1912–1999), the authoritative Japanese translator of *In Buddha's Words*.

It was challenging for us to translate *In Buddha's Words* into English, as we are now twice-removed from the Pali-language original. For example, the lines quoted in this poem come from what Nakamura refers to as the "Rhinoceros Horn Sutra," but we learned that English-language scholars of early Buddhism drop the word "horn," opting to call this sutra the "Rhinoceros Sutra."

"Is It December Again?"

The final poem in the book relies heavily on the Japanese verb *yureru*, which appears seven times in the poem. There are many translation candidates for *yureru*: quake, pitch, rock, sway, swing, toss, tremble, vacillate, vibrate, jolt, joggle, swing, waver, flicker. Hirata evokes the different meanings of *yureru* by replacing the initial *kanji* character with a *hiragana* lettering, thereby intentionally obscuring its meaning and allowing for numerous interpretations.

The voice of the bus driver, who uses the verb *yureru* three times in the poem, was also challenging. A bus driver delivering polite verbal warnings is typical in Japan, but bus drivers in the U.S. are not nearly so polite, so we had to develop an authentic way for the driver to speak in English. "Rough road up ahead" was one way we translated *yureru* without needing to use a verb at all: "rough road" captures the *yureru*-ing, as well as the sense of a journey.

In preparing to translate this poem, we read an excellent English translation and analysis by Carol Hayes and Rina Kikuchi published by the Institute for Economic and Business Research, Shiga University. Hayes and Kikuchi's translated version, titled "The Seventh of the Twenty-Fourth Month," gets into deeper exposition of the word *michiyuki*. We agree with their analysis that the word *michiyuki* could be referring to a suicide pact between star-crossed lovers—in this case, the lovers being the speaker and the goldfish. In our version, in order to honor Hirata's lighthearted, humorous intent, we translated *michiyukji* as "journey." We went as a far as to translate the proper name, Michuyuki, as "Journey" in order to reinforce the theme of a journey coming to its end. We feel this whole poem reflects back on the first lines of the first poem in the book, in which Hirata begins, "I'm going on a trip / Just to write poetry."

"Is It December Again?" ends with a new journey beginning and an existential question: "Will we die?   Will we survive?"

Acknowledgments

"Is It November?" and "Is It February Again?" by Hirata Toshiko, translated from the Japanese by Eric E. Hyett and Spencer Thurlow, in *Pendemics* (Issue 2, Spring, 2021)

"Is It July?" and "Is It August?" by Hirata Toshiko, translated from the Japanese by Eric E. Hyett and Spencer Thurlow, in the *Georgia Review* (February 2021)

"Is It January?" and "Is It January Again?" by Hirata Toshiko, translated from the Japanese by Eric E. Hyett and Spencer Thurlow, in *Modern Poetry in Translation* (2020 Number 1)

"Is It March Again?" and "Is it May Again?" by Hirata Toshiko, translated from the Japanese by Eric E. Hyett and Spencer Thurlow, in *Granta* (November 2020)

"Is It October?" by Hirata Toshiko, translated from the Japanese by Eric E. Hyett and Spencer Thurlow, in *World Literature Today* (Autumn 2020)

"Is It February?" "Is It March?" "Is It November Again?" and "Is It December Again?" by Hirata Toshiko, translated from the Japanese by Eric E. Hyett and Spencer Thurlow, in *Transference,* Western Michigan University (Summer 2020)

"Is it September Again?" "Is It July Again?" "Is It June?" "Is It April?" "Is it August Again?" and "Is it October Again?" by Hirata Toshiko, translated from the Japanese by Eric E. Hyett and Spencer Thurlow, in *Tokyo Poetry Journal* (Summer 2020)

Hirata Toshiko is one of Japan's most notable contemporary poets with ten volumes of poetry in print. She also writes novels, plays, and essays. She first became known during the "women's boom" in contemporary Japanese literature in the 1980s, along with Hiromi Itō and others. Her collection *Shinanoka* (Tokyo, Shichōsha, 2004, now available in English as *Is It Poetry?*) earned Hirata the Hagiwara Sakutarō Prize for poetry.

Spencer Thurlow's poetry or translations have appeared in the *Georgia Review, Granta, Cincinnati Review, Worcester Review*, and others. With Eric Hyett, Spencer cotranslated Sonic Peace by Kiriu Minashita (Phoneme Media, 2017) and *Is It Poetry?* (Phoneme Media/Deep Vellum, 2024). Sonic Peace was shortlisted for the American Literary Translators Association's 2018 National Translation Award, as well as the Lucien Stryk Prize for Asian Translation. He served as poet laureate of West Tisbury 2018–2022.

Eric Hyett is a poet, writer, and Japanese translator from Brookline, Massachusetts, U.S.A. His first book of poetry, *Aporia*, was published in 2022 (Lily Poetry Review Books). Eric's poetry also appears in magazines and journals such as the *Worcester Review, Cincinnati Review, Barrow Street*, the *Hudson Review*, and *Harvard Review Online*. With Spencer Thurlow, Eric cotranslated *Sonic Peace* by Kiriu Minashita (Phoneme Media, 2017) and *Is It Poetry?* (Phoneme Media/ Deep Vellum, 2024).